Inspire!

fresh ideas for creative youth work

Nigel Pimlott
Jo Pimlott
Dave Wiles

WITHDRAWN

© Jo Pimlott, Nigel Pimlott, Dave Wiles 2001
First published 2002

Scripture Union, 207–209 Queensway, Bletchley,
Milton Keynes, MK2 2EB, England
www.scriptureunion.org.uk

ISBN 1 85999 429 6

British Library Cataloguing-in-Publication Data.
A catalogue record of this book is available from the British Library.

Printed and bound in Great Britain by Creative Print and Design (Wales)
Ebbw Vale.

Scripture Union is an international Christian charity working with
churches in more than 130 countries, providing resources to bring the
good news about Jesus Christ to children, young people and families
and to encourage them to develop spiritually through the Bible and
prayer.

As well as our network of volunteers, staff and associates who run
holidays, church-based events and school Christian groups, we produce
a wide range of publications and support those who use our resources
through training programmes.

Contents

This resource is made up of a book and a CD-ROM. The CD-ROM is full of ideas for working with young people. The CD contains five resource packs on the subjects of Easter, Christmas, Freedom, Identity and Belonging. Each includes games, activities, discussion starters, stories, poems and visual images.

Each pack can be used in a flexible manner so the young people you work with can get the most from the material. Combined with the tools in the book – group work, participation and creativity – the packs form an exciting resource for both the youth worker and young people.

There is no prescriptive way dictating how they should be used. They are designed to be adapted to meet the needs of individual groups.

Appropriate for use with both Christian and not-yet-Christian young people, the CD-ROM tackles issues which concern young people.

Inspire!

This project would not have been possible without the help of a number of people. Our thanks and appreciation go to them all.

Claire Bell
Sue Budden
Bernie Comissiong
Terry Dunnell
Michael Eastman
Mark Garside
Ben Holloway
David Howlett
Lucie Hutson
Neil Hutson
David Montgomery
John Pawley
Keith Pentelow
Matt Smart
Heather Wright

Introduction

My late father-in-law was excellent at making things with his hands. He built his own house, was well-trained in woodwork and there were few things he couldn't mend or turn his hand to. He taught me many skills and tricks of the trade. He also taught me that without the right tools, many jobs are impossible. He had a tool for every eventuality; tools you would use every day and tools you would only use once or twice in a lifetime. Some tools enabled work to be done which otherwise would require employing expensive professionals. If a tool existed, the chances were he would possess it.

For people working with young people, there are many natural 'tools' to hand – such as our ability to love and care for young people, befriend and encourage them, challenge and inspire them. There are other 'tools' which are more about the techniques used in work with young people. These techniques are picked up through experience, yet rarely are we formally taught them.

The purpose of this book is to pass on some of the basic tools for working with young people in Bible study groups, youth groups and other settings where they are looking for spiritual development and growth in the Christian faith. This book is not a step-by-step 'how to...' manual, but a collection of tools to carry out the work – tools to help with group work, creativity and full and active participation. It is hoped that these will inspire you in your work with young people.

Working

with

Groups

of Young

People

Working with Groups of Young People

Nigel Pimlott

The challenge of groups

Anyone who has been in youth work for any length of time will know that working in groups can be one of the most rewarding aspects. That sense of planning a programme, preparing and praying through the agenda, and then seeing the young people excited and empowered as they unpack the programme and take on board ownership of the ideas and concepts is truly fulfilling. To see them develop ideas, initiative and the confidence to deliver their own material is at the very heart of discipling and releasing young people.

It would be great if every session with young people worked out this way. Sadly, it doesn't. Often youth workers are tired, short of time, ideas and resources, and under pressure from the young people, their parents and their church!

Every group of young people is different. What works with one set of teenagers may not work with another. A great discussion had by a group of girls may flop dismally with a bunch of lads. The environments of the village and the city are very different and often different approaches are needed. It would be impossible to provide a set of suggestions and guidelines for every type of group in every situation in a book of this size.

What follows are some general principles for effective group work with teenagers. These seek to enable the young people to maximise their learning, potential and enjoyment.

The main aim of this chapter is to provide encouragement and confidence building ideas and techniques for those relatively new to youth work. At the same time, we hope it will be helpful for experienced youth workers who may wish to refresh their knowledge and skills.

The leader's role

Leadership style

There are two basic components in working with groups: the group and those leading or facilitating the group. It is not the purpose of this book to do an in-depth analysis of styles and types of leadership. There is so much written on this subject that to add to it would be duplication. A basic overview is, however, provided along with some pointers to help the process of facilitation.

Whether you are an autocratic, democratic or very passive leader, the goals of church leadership are the same: to help those in the group be and achieve all that God has in store for them. In our very fluid culture, flexibility and adaptability are key components to working with young people.

Some groups of young people are led by one adult, some by a team of adults, some by the young people themselves and others by a combination of young people and adults. Some groups may be run by a committee, some by an outside body (like a parachurch organisation), some by consensus of opinion and, perhaps the worst-case scenario, some are not led at all!

...to help those in the group be and achieve all that God has in store for them.

Some youth leaders prefer to have an 'event' led programme for the group they work with, whilst others are focused more on relationships. Whilst it is perhaps unfair to say that this is a 'one or the other' situation, we all have needs, in varying degrees, for affirmation and affiliation and our styles of leadership may well reflect our own needs.

Whatever your own personal needs, style or preferences, it is my belief that, in working with groups of young people, it is essential that some degree of balance and diversity exists within the overall youth team. Wherever possible, my advice would be to work as a team rather than individuals and to assess the strengths and weaknesses of those individuals within any team, taking account of any imbalances as appropriate.

Common ground

Whether you know the group you are working with or they are new to you, relationships with young people have to be worked on and developed. Working from a position of common ground is both a good starting point and excellent for continual development. This may be obvious, but it is because it's so obvious that it can sometimes be overlooked.

It could be that a sports team, a favourite music group or a CD, or a Playstation game is the common ground which helps bridge gaps between yourself and the young people. One of the young guys I work with always reviews his latest CD purchase with me. We swap albums and share experiences, which helps deepen our relationship. When we then meet in a group together, the conversation flows easily.

There mustn't be any sense of falseness or manipulation about doing this. I genuinely enjoy much of the music young people like and am always up for a conversation about football or Playstations (perhaps I have never grown up). Try and find subjects where you can bridge gaps and enjoy conversations both within and outside the formal group environment.

Animator

In the past a group facilitator has sometimes been referred to as a catalyst for the group. Whilst this may be accurate as a description, it is not the best way of facilitating a group of young people. The problem with a catalyst is that although it effects change, it remains unchanged itself in the function it performs. A more effective way of working could be described as being an animator.

An animator brings life and movement to a group whilst at the same time being changed themselves. I do not believe it is possible to work effectively with young people without being changed ourselves. Our perceptions, expectations and ideas about how God works should be constantly challenged as the young people outwork their relationship with God in the context of their culture. We must adapt, develop and always seek the new thing God is about.

My own spiritual journey has reflected this process many times. All too often I have prepared something for a particular event or youth work session, only to find that when I arrive to do the a session, God is already on the case. He has been at work independently of my efforts!

From time to time, I have worked with a group of young people from a church in the Midlands. The first time I met them, I led the worship and they nervously joined in. At our next meeting, I prepared the worship, expecting to lead it as before. To my surprise, it was the young people who led the worship.

They did it creatively, passionately and better than I would have done. Our journey together changed my perception of them. My expectation was that they wouldn't be up to the job, but the seeds sown from our previous times together and their hard work changed them and changed my view.

Animation is about stimulating the mental, physical, emotional and spiritual life of individuals so that they can undertake a wider range of activities gaining greater degrees of awareness, fulfillment and belonging to the group they are part of.

Empowerment

To empower is to 'give power to, make able, to authorise, to license'. Young people need empowering if they are to be all that God intended them to be.

Having done all your preparations, it can be frustrating when the group takes your carefully prepared material off in a different direction. We will discuss this further later, but this is one of the possible consequences of true empowerment.

To give young people the licence and authority to do their own thing in the group is both rewarding and risky: rewarding in that young people can grow and develop, and risky in that they can go to places you have not been before. Some youth workers and church leaders are not prepared to take such a risk. The stifling of such initiative can only lead to the group being less vitalised and complete than it otherwise might have been.

The skills required from youth workers to empower young people take time to develop. To set sail in uncharted spiritual waters is both exciting and demanding. The conclusions of such empowerment may be surprising, but nevertheless valuable in the rich tapestry of the Kingdom of God.

A number of people in the church I go to have befriended a group of lads who are into skateboarding. They have a skate park in the town but it is in need of repair and improvement. Rather than try and tell them what needs to be done, the team from the church have sought to empower the young people. They have encouraged them to take responsibility and try and obtain funding for the project themselves.

> If you are not used to empowering a group of young people and letting go of the reins, try it and see what happens. You may be surprised.

All the interested parties have formed a management group to do this, with the young people, members of the local council, voluntary sector and the church all involved. Increasingly, it is the young people who are moving the process forward.

There is inevitably a tension between leading a group and allowing it to 'self-learn'. Observation over many years would suggest that leading is only good if people are following. The lessons learnt from being led are not as easily remembered and put into practice as those lessons learnt through self-discovery and personal experience, which are sometimes painful, but ultimately beneficial.

If you are not used to empowering a group of young people and letting go of the reins, try it and see what happens. You may be surprised.

Self-awareness

Whatever type of leader you are, the group will have a perception of you. Your level of skill, personality, knowledge, depth of relationships will all be informally assessed by your very astute group of young people. They will quickly suss out if you are trying to be something you are not and will form an opinion about you.

There is no point trying to be something you are not. Be yourself and be aware of who you are. Assess your strengths and weaknesses in your group work and work with young people. If you are not so strong in one particular area, try and work with others who have complementary gifts and personality traits. There are many ways of achieving the same results.

> There is no point trying to be something you are not. Be yourself and be aware of who you are.

Many voluntary youth workers can feel that they are not good enough to work with young people and confidence can sometimes be low. Don't let this stop you engaging with young people. They need role models, adult friends, people to laugh with, eat with and share joy and pain with. All these things are evident themselves in groups, large or small. Every youth worker has started somewhere, and all have stories to tell of when things went wrong.

The more you work with groups of young people, the more you will gain in experience and confidence. Learn from others who have been there before you, learn from the young people and develop relationships with them. They will learn to value and appreciate you for who you are. In a world that is so often superficial and cosmetic, they are looking and longing for reality and meaningful relationships.

Try working with your group in different ways. Involve them in the experiments. Inform them that you are trying something new and would appreciate their help. From the CD-ROM materials, pick out something you would not normally tackle. Undertake the piece of work, see how it goes and then review it with the young people afterwards. By doing this, you will have a greater understanding of how well something worked and gain in skill, whilst the young people will feel much more involved if you seek and value their opinion on how well things have gone.

Knowledge and responsibility

There can be a tendency when working with a group of young people to think that you have to know everything. This can be particularly true if the group is new to you. This can produce a lot of pressure and lead to tension in the group especially if you try and bluff your way out of a situation! There is no need to do this.

A group of lads I work with think I am the fount of all wisdom on particular subjects. They are deluded! I don't know how this situation has come about, but it is a tag I sometimes get embarrassed about. Deeper reflection has highlighted a few clues as to why they think this.

It is not because I know the answers to the questions they often ask, but it could be because I will often say 'I don't know the answer to that one'. It could be because I sometimes say that I don't know, but I will try and find out or ask someone who might know. It could be because I will admit my own failings and weaknesses and search for answers and truth.

It is all right to say we don't know. It is acceptable to ask a question in response to a question. In his book *Mentoring for Mission*, Gunter Krallman tells a wonderful story about a Rabbi. The Rabbi's disciples (his group if you like) were always troubled that the Rabbi would often respond to one question with another question. One day they plucked up courage to challenge the Rabbi. 'Rabbi?' they asked, 'Why do you always reply to one of our questions with a question of your own?' The Rabbi replied, 'So what's wrong with a question?'.

Having said that we do not need to know everything, we should have a sense of responsibility for all that we are, say and do. Amongst the knowledge that we do possess must be a core understanding of the Gospel and the Good News of the Kingdom. Jesus instructs us very clearly not to cause 'the little ones to stumble' (Matthew 18:6). I have heard some horrendous things communicated by youth workers to groups of young people.

If you do get into deep water, don't be afraid to pause, reflect and say that you will come back to that later to tackle it individually at a more appropriate time. Don't use this as a cop out, but do what you say you will do. You will be respected and valued as part of the group all the more for it.

Watch your language

Whether your group is 800 young people in a school assembly or three young people in a front room, you need to watch your language. Too often youth workers presume that young people understand what they are talking about. This is aptly illustrated by the vicar who waxed lyrical in a school about the Levites, only to leave the pupils wondering why he was talking about jeans!

Equally, it is not good to patronise the group you are working with. A balance must be sought between the two extremes. I do not believe that our language has to be complex in order to communicate complex ideas. In fact, the best form of communication is to explain complicated ideas simply and clearly.

Young people like to explore and we must do all we can to help them. Even the best youth workers use inappropriate language from time to time. Why not negotiate an agreement with the group you are working with to stop you and ask you to explain every time you say something they don't understand? You will be amazed how quickly you learn to be more apt. If you work as part of a team, invite the team to listen to how you communicate and make a note of the things you have said which could be misunderstood. Again you will be a quick learner.

Planning

Many youth workers wrestle with the 'tyranny of the immediate': that sudden realisation that you have a group to facilitate tonight and you haven't done any preparation. In our busy and stressful world, preparation is one of the first casualties. The problem is that poor preparation can lead to unfulfilled potential and often to disappointment on the part of the young people.

Unless we are prepared to make the sacrifice of the time demanded by preparation and recognise that there is a cost in working with young people, we are in danger of selling our young people short and ending up with disillusionment. Perhaps this is why surveys suggest people only stay in youth work for a relatively short period of time – on average only 18–24 months.

Who is in the group?

One individual can transform a group of young people both for the better and for the worse! Every individual brings with them gifts, potential and valuable experiences, but also baggage from the past, the traumas of the day and their family situation. We need to pay attention to these things. Awareness of individual needs may well help to avoid catastrophe in the group.

Peter always demands attention. If he doesn't get it he will be disruptive, confrontational and, it has to be said, very annoying. In one-to-one conversations, Peter always tells you when he is next going to see his mum. She left a couple of years ago and he lives with his dad. This is why he needs special love and attention. When taking a group with Peter in it, part of the planning is to make sure that he will be accommodated as an individual without compromising or neglecting others in the group.

Individuals may bring other factors into the group which need special attention in the planning stages. Negative family situations, relationships or sexual experiences need to be borne in mind when discussing certain subject matters. Racial and gender issues need to be thought through with sensitivity and consideration. The spiritual and emotional maturity of the group needs to be taken on board. Presumption is a dangerous place to work from.

Aims and objectives

It has become a cliché in management training circles that if you 'aim at nothing you will hit nothing', but it is true! Having being involved for many years in training others to work with young people, I am constantly surprised at how many group sessions and activities are planned entirely from a topic-led perspective, with survival and entertainment being the only criteria for the success of the session.

It is my firm belief that we need to ask some bigger questions:

▌ What am I trying to achieve with this group of young people?
▌ How will this help them?
▌ How will this session I am planning, fit into the bigger picture of my youth work?
▌ Do I have a vision, an aim, a strategy which can be identified?

■ Do my principles and beliefs run through my plan for this session? (eg is there participation by the young people, is it creative, is it culturally relevant etc.)

■ What outcome am I hoping to be able to quantify by the end of the session?

■ How will I (and the young people) know if success has been achieved?

Sorry if this is obvious to some, but it is sadly ignored by many. According to Abraham Maslow's *Hierarchy of Needs Model*, self-fulfilment is the ultimate goal of human needs. Whilst our motivation for working with young people should not be selfish, it is nice to feel fulfilled. I do not meet many youth workers who radiate this sense of fulfillment and satisfaction. Often it is because they do not have a clear sense of what they are trying to be and do. They could not excite others in this process because of a lack of clarity and couldn't say whether they are doing a good job or not.

The very worst that can happen if we establish clear aims and objectives is that we know we have failed. The good thing about failing is that we can start again, make adjustments and work towards success. The best that can happen is that we are happy and content and the young people are engaged with God, us and one another.

Involve the young people

Effective planning should help your group run smoothly. I see far too many youth workers trying to do everything themselves. It seems as though the busier individuals get, the more they try and do everything and the less they delegate. Not only does this eventually cripple them, it stops the young people growing and being involved.

I love to involve the young people in the planning process. I notice that they often need time to think things over, but once they have grabbed hold of things, they will fly. Break down the tasks you think need doing and ask the young people help deliver them. Try and match their skills, gifts and interests to what you are asking and offer to help and guide them.

Initially, this requires an investment of time for little return and sometimes it doesn't all go to plan. Given time and grace to make mistakes, the young people will rise to the challenge, produce great group work themselves and cut your workload! I know which of our young people will prepare a great talk, dance, drama, game, piece of worship or discussion stimulus. I no longer need to monitor closely what they do in the preparation stage as they are now used to the processes. The product is normally first class and these are 14- and 15-year-olds!

Venue

Some youth work activities are tied to a particular venue, whilst others are not. If you have some flexibility why not try and experiment a little with the venues you use. Running a discussion with half a dozen young people in a dull church building doesn't seem the best way of creating a good environment. Try using a someone's lounge or garden. The same material prepared in the same way can work differently in different environments.

Don't get stuck in the mire of tradition. Just because you have always met in the same place, at the same time, on the same day doesn't mean that it's the best place, time or day. Take a look at what you are doing and ask whether the venue you are using is the best for the aims and objectives you have.

Length of meeting

In a similar way, the length of time that your group is together can affect the outcomes of group work. The church I am part of recently ran some small group meetings for the lads in the church. The sessions lasted for a exactly an hour. They were high impacting, concentrated and concise. The sessions were then changed to an hour and a half (at the young people's request, which raises some more questions about knowledge and responsibility) and have now become a little drawn out, fragmented and static.

Before the change, everyone turned up on time and there was a shared responsibility in doing this. Now people drift in and out, which has destabilised the group. Again, ask the question: are you meeting for the right length of time?

Asking the right questions

When we first undertake work with a group, our own nervousness and inexperience can be one of our biggest handicaps. The preparation of material has gone well, but the delivery to the group has not. The ten hours of prepared material has evaporated within three minutes and you now have an hour to fill and nothing to fill it with! Thinking about how you pose questions will not only bring variety and structure to the group work, but also help you deliver them.

Closed questions

A series of 'yes' and 'no' answers to a string of questions is usually not very constructive, but is sometimes a good starting point. The question 'Did you enjoy the church meeting on Sunday?' will probably produce a short answer, but the short answer can be developed further to produce discussion. This type of question is particularly good at making people feel at ease, but shouldn't be used too frequently once a rapport has been established in the group. It is then better to use other types of questions to draw out opinion and different contributions.

Open questions

'How?', 'What?', 'Where?' and 'When?' are all examples of open questions. They demand more than a one word answer and are the basis for all our conversations. Not only do these types of question open up a topic for conversation, they also have an additional benefit in group work. The nature of these questions means that the individual who provides the answer is in control of how much information and detail they give to the group. This can aid feelings of security and develop trust within a group setting. The use of further questions can draw out deeper feelings and opinions, but the ultimate decision of disclosure rests with the individual. The potential drawback regarding this type of question is that the conversation can go off track.

'What did you enjoy about the church meeting on Sunday?'
'How did you feel about the church meeting on Sunday?'

Leading questions

'Wasn't the church meeting on Sunday great?' is an example of a leading question. It demands a response and the question usually originates from the group leader's own feelings and opinions, disregarding the young people's views. This type of question can be quite destructive if used inappropriately by the group leader.

The group can be controlled and manipulated, and individuals can feel belittled and patronised. I have found one positive use of this type of question, when playing the role of devil's advocate in a discussion. A little bit of provocation and winding up (not that I would ever do such a thing!) can be a great way of stimulating teenagers and producing great debates and discussions.

Probing questions

If relationships are good, there is sometimes a call to delve a little deeper into an answer given by an individual. 'You seem to have disliked the meeting on Sunday, but I don't know why. Could you tell me more?' is an example of such a probing question. These types of questions sometimes need to be used to help those in the group who are a little low on confidence.

Often, you can sense that a young person has an important contribution to make, but they cannot find the words or confidence to present their views. A little help and probing from you will help them in their development.

Appropriate illustrations

Whilst not specifically a type of question, illustrations are an important tool in working with groups. If you pose the question, 'Who can recall a Sunday church meeting which they particularly enjoyed?' to a group of young people, you may not get a response. However, if you provide an illustration and tell a story about a meeting you enjoyed this may well lead to others opening up.

Whilst Sunday meetings are not highly personal subjects for most people, other topics need to be treated more sensitively. Disclosing personal information can be embarrassing and costly for a young person. They may be bullied or teased later on. A colleague who works with young offenders tells me they are unwilling to discuss anything of a personal nature in a group situation. However, if they are given a hypothetical, prepared scenario, then they are very happy to join in the discussion. Video clips, problem-page letters and role plays are good ways of providing such illustrations, giving people a 'safe' way of expressing themselves.

When things go off track

Times of testing

If you are new to a group, there may well be a time of testing and probing by the young people as they check you out and search for a level of relationship. This is an important time and it is essential that you establish their trust and gain a mutual sense of respect.

The young people may set some tests especially for you they try to gauge where you are at. These can be trying times for youth workers, but be patient as perseverance through these times will bring a reward for both you and the young people.

There will always be occasions when a particular piece of work doesn't quite work out as you had hoped – when things dry up and no one will participate. We've probably all been in the position of observing a group of young people talk and chat away in the informality of an evening. As soon as something formal is started, complete silence descends on the group and no one will say anything. Amazingly, we witness the talk and freedom resume once the more formal part of the evening has stopped.

Sometimes the opposite happens and the discussion is so intense and excitable that you end up way off the point and are left helplessly floundering, trying to focus the group. Don't get paranoid! This is part of normal life and it is part of adolescent development and interpersonal dynamics. Except in extreme and rare cases, it is unlikely to be anything you or your fellow youth workers have done. Ask any parent!

Focus

Having planned your session, you know exactly where you want it to go. The problem is that the young people want it to go somewhere else. All your attempts to keep the session on track appear to be failing. Every time you make a serious point, one of the sharper young people replies with a snappy one-liner which has the group in fits of laughter and leaves you looking stupid.

Handling these sorts of situations is one of the major challenges in youth work. Learning when to go with the flow and when to focus and concentrate are key skills. The spiritual development of young people is not a simple process, but a complex and variable one. In a classroom environment, control can be more easily exercised, but in the youth-group setting different techniques have to be employed.

Letting go and pulling back

Sometimes we do have to abandon our plan and go with the flow. Sometimes God does want to run a different agenda to ours and we need to know when these times are. Sometimes we need to negotiate with the young people. There is more than one way to achieve your aims and objectives. The Spirit can work in the most mysterious of ways. I recall one session my wife and I were leading with a group unfamiliar to us. One lad was boasting about his ability to handle conflict and how he saw himself as the 'policeman' of the young people in his town. He was the kingpin and wouldn't hesitate to use violence to combat bullying in the name of justice and rights for all.

We were talking about conflict and his general attitude was one of 'I get them before they get me'. At the same time he was proclaiming what a great faith he had. The rest of the group was watching and you could sense they were waiting to see how we would respond. After much banter and discussion, a few role plays and some games, this guy was in control of the group. He continued to boast about his seemingly divine right to be judge, jury and executioner.

The session was slipping away from us until my wife said very bluntly, 'the Bible calls that sin'. My wife was not prone to such outbursts and is normally the master of diplomacy. Silence fell upon the group and tension filled the church hall. To cut the story short, this word of 'wisdom' cut through the bravado and revealed a hurting young man who sat with his local youth leader until the early hours, talking through why he was like he was. A few days later, we were thanked for being so honest and helping this guy to be set free from some of his personal insecurities.

It takes time to know when to let go and when to pull back. Deep down, young people are usually very gracious and tolerant (though it may not seem like it on the surface sometimes) if they know that you are for them. Often we have to use the momentum they provide to shape what happens in a group. I understand that this is the basic skill involved in Judo: allowing force and momentum to work for you and not against you.

When silence is not golden

There are possibly too few moments of silence in our busy, frantic world. Unfortunately, the periods of silence we do encounter can sometimes be embarrassing and tense affairs. Something has 'gone off' just before the group meet and everyone is in a bad mood. Each young person decides that this would be a good time to comply with the adolescent stereotype of moodiness, rebellion and antagonism. Silence has set in. All people are different and young people are no exceptions. Some are shy, others feel ignored, rejected, bored and frustrated, and sometimes they can take it all out on you. In these situations it is important to stay calm and try and respond in the opposite spirit. Be open, polite, patient and give the young people choices about what to do.

Working with groups of young people can be stressful and it can sometimes feel like it is you against them. If this happens, try and diffuse the situation with some humour or some food! Occasionally, I have just waited to see what happens, complementing the silence with my own. You have to be wise in doing this, but sometimes it works and the young people can begin to deal with the situation they find themselves in.

Perhaps the best way of working in this type of environment is to:

▌ be very specific in what you ask the young people to do
▌ break down your group into smaller groups

- involve those who want to be involved
- chat to individuals who are struggling
- do some ice-breaking activities to create some openness.

Dominant individuals

In contrast, the very dominant individual is also hard to cope with. They are keen to answer every question, have an opinion on every topic, have been there, done that and no one else's opinions are really important. The rest of the group can easily cease to function and then they can slip into 'turn off' mode and fall asleep.

Sometimes, the dominant individual can have a clown or joker mentality. Every comment has a witty remark attached to it, or someone is poked fun at and the general level of the group work is lowered. These individuals can be very frustrating for the group leader.

> Maybe they are starved of love and attention, maybe they are overcompensating for their low self-esteem, or maybe they are just extreme extroverts.

It is so important that we look at why individuals behave in these ways. Maybe they are starved of love and attention, maybe they are overcompensating for low self-esteem, or maybe they are just extreme extroverts. Whatever the reasons, they need to be treated with love and patience.

It is often a good idea to try and incorporate the rest of the group into a discussion if one individual is very dominant. Ask the rest of the group what they think about the answer the dominant young person has just given. This draws in the group and also makes it clear to the individual that this is a time for others to speak. Sometimes you can interject your own views, emotions and opinions to draw in others. Breaking down into smaller groups can also aid more contributions and prevent one person being totally dominant.

Taking time

If things go seriously off track and you see no benefit in the diversion, don't be afraid to take a break. Have a drink and come back to things later. Alternatively, play a quick game to change the atmosphere or offer to pick certain things up at a later date when you have had time to think and prepare more on the topic of discussion.

Be willing to listen and to learn even in the most unconstructive of times. Often someone will say something significanct, which can be developed as a thought, allowing the group to move on to something more constructive. If someone in the group is making a point, don't rush on and leave their contribution in mid-air. Give it respect and significance. It is very tempting to ask a question and then ignore all the answers until you hear the one you wanted.

> If someone in the group is making a point, don't rush on and leave their contribution in midair. Give it respect and significance.

This often happens in family services or Sunday school environments. The answers young people give are passed over until the 'one and only' answer is shouted out. Most things in life have several answers. What often happens in groups where the leader adopts this style is that the young people learn to give the answer that the leader is looking for. This is uncreative, stifling and only benefits the ego of the leader. It does nothing for the young people.

In the past, I have worked with adult prisoners and young offenders. I love these environments because they often do not give the answers you would expect or that other groups of people in society would give. This challenges our thinking and theology and should stop us making simplistic inane statements that experience does not support. Young people need to own and believe in what they are doing and saying, if it is to have value and purpose.

Boundaries

Setting the ground rules

Many good youth initiatives are destroyed by disruptive and antisocial behaviour. One fight, one relationship conflict, a family argument spilling over into the group, or substance abuse can wreak havoc in a group. Sometimes we are afraid to set boundaries, fearing that they will not encourage people to be part of a group. My experience would indicate the opposite. Young people work best within boundaries, as they bring safety and security into their world which is often an unsafe and insecure one.

Again, balance is the key to successful boundary setting, and one of the best ways of accomplishing this is to let the young people set their own boundaries. Let them decide what is and what is not acceptable. Run a session on this subject and allow discussion and debate to filter some of the more extreme and wacky ideas which are sure to surface. Invite the young people to prioritise or vote on which boundaries and rules they wish to see established. You will be amazed how effective such a process can be. The young people can also decide on the consequences of exceeding the boundaries.

Safety

Some young people are very vulnerable and feel uncomfortable doing certain activities. In one of the groups I work with, some of the girls have been tremendously reluctant to go swimming. Society and image pressures have made them feel desperately insecure about revealing parts of their bodies by wearing swimsuits. In such cases, we need to provide ways in which young people can opt out without feeling they are excluded.

Alternative safe places need to be created within our groups so that a culture of safety can be fostered. Keep a special look out for those on the edges who are perhaps not behaving as you might expect. Don't put too much pressure on them to conform: there may be something serious going on below the surface which accounts for their behaviour.

As a group dynamic develops, conversations will prosper and confidentiality will need to be respected. Inexperienced youth leaders – especially young ones – don't always handle pieces of sensitive information in the most appropriate ways. It is not the purpose of this book to have a full discussion on the issues of child protection, The Children's Act and how to handle disclosures by young people, but do take time to understand and implement your church's or denomination's procedures and guidelines.

How to go deeper

All is well

Assuming your group is going well and the material you are using is proving suitable, some seriously deep issues and emotions may well come to the surface. Sometime this causes fear in the group leader and wisdom is called for, but this is where I believe the best youth work can take place: with real issues in the reality of the culture the young people find themselves in.

Much of the material accompanying this pack is designed to get to those real issues and the realities they present. Much of the field testing we have carried out has confirmed and endorsed this approach. Many young people carry deep hurts and concerns and you may well be the only person who is trying to talk to them about these concerns. Don't knock them back, but gently try to help them. As we have discussed, some issues may need picking up in another environment but, equally, some may be best dealt with in a group setting, particularly where the individual is comfortable in the group.

There have been many occasions where a young person has said something which has stilled the group: a piece of personal and painful information that everyone has identified with. If this happens, it is vital that you help the young person. The teams I have worked with have often consisted of younger and less experienced leaders, and usually they will look to the senior leader to take a lead in these situations. This is okay as they will watch and learn how to handle groups in these circumstances.

Vulnerability

Some models of leadership teach isolation from the crowd and a 'holier than thou' type of attitude. This was not modelled by Jesus. He made himself vulnerable and we should do the same. Young people will respond positively to your story and be encouraged to tell theirs.

At the time of writing, my wife and I cannot have children. We have been open with the young people we work with about this and in turn they have encouraged and supported us. I am convinced that we will reap what we sow. If we are guarded and secretive, I think it unlikely we will develop deep and meaningful relationships with the young people in our groups.

In our home town, the young people have seen us in their school being honest and open. Because of this, then, they feel comfortable telling us their deepest concerns, sometimes in the middle of the street.

Activity
Young people usually talk more freely if they are doing something. Cooking, washing up, putting out chairs or packing away the PA equipment can all be good occasions to have deep and meaningful conversations with members of the group you lead. Some of our most enlightening discussions have taken place on car journeys, where often the young people will chat away and forget we are there at all.

These activities can be places of common ground where there are no fences between you and the young person. Particularly after a rousing session, the young people may wish to chat further or unpack something that they have been doing during the session which has taken place. Making the coffee can be a great environment for this to take place.

Maintaining momentum

Sitting back or pressing forward?
In our busy and stressful lives, it is sometimes too easy to sit back and enjoy the ride. Having done great pieces of group work with the young people and excited, encouraged and challenged them, the easy life can be tempting. The lure of the armchair or the PC can be attractive.

If the group you work with is to continue to grow and develop, progress must always be monitored and evaluated. One of the quickest ways to become stagnant is to stay where you are, with the mindset you have always had and using techniques you have always used. If there is an overriding message to be learnt from church history, it is this: God is a God who interacts with humanity, He is doing new things in new ways and if we are not flexible and settle for what we have, we will probably lose it. There is always a new challenge with God.

Welcoming newcomers?

In some of the groups I work with, there is a tendency for cliques to develop amongst the young people. These act as barriers to others wanting to join the group and it is one of the major challenges of the leader to balance being sympathetic to the existing group dynamic and welcoming to the newcomer.

I do not believe hospitality just happens, it has to be worked on. The area I live in is very territorial and doesn't take kindly to outside influences. I could see Jesus telling the story of the Good Samaritan in my community, with its positive dislike of outsiders. This outworks itself in many of the young people in the church and it needs working on to create an environment which reflects the values of Christianity. It is something which needs to be monitored as we seek to move forward.

Not again

There can be few things as frustrating as doing a lot of preparatory work, with hours of study and prayer (OK minutes), focusing on the task in hand and then two or three people turn up when you had planned for a dozen or so. If we are looking to maintain momentum in our work with young people, we cannot treat the time the group is together as our only responsibility.

Some churches opt for a heavy-handed approach with monitoring of attendance, whilst others are so laid back that no one is ever phoned to see if there is a problem or asked if everything is all right. Somewhere in the middle is a balance which shows a caring, pastoral heart for the individual and keeps the bigger picture of the working of the group in mind.

I always encourage the young people in the groups I work with to telephone and encourage each other. It's just good communication and creates a sense of community.

Consequences of growth

If your group of young people grows significantly in numbers, then it is more than likely that you will have to adopt a new strategy. The group of ten that once met in your front room is now up to thirty-six and they are hanging from the light fittings. Change is difficult for all of us, but for young people searching for purpose and identity and perhaps coming from an unstable home situation, a change in group structure can be traumatic.

I have observed that however successfully such changes are managed, some young people don't cope with the well and drift away. When the church I belong to moved from a youth club environment to a cell-based structure we lost several young people. We can, however, attempt to make such changes as smooth as possible by involving the young people in the process, concentrating on relationships rather than structures and having personal conversations with as many of the group as possible.

How do you disciple the young people ?

Whatever and however we choose to do things, the issue of discipleship should be at the heart of all that we are about. It is this biblical pattern of helping others grow, mentoring, training and releasing which will, above all else, produce successful groups of young people.

It is easy to lose sight of what we are really all about: loving, caring, ministering to and receiving ministry from the young people we work alongside. It is when these factors are flowing that we will find our work most rewarding and satisfying.

Participation

Participation

Dave Wiles

Why participation?

The participation of young people is not an easy option for youth workers who want to avoid preparation. If anything the implementation of effective participation with young people is more time consuming and requires us to draw upon our creativity and group-work skills in new ways. However, I should say from the outset that I believe that an inclusive style of working with young people is the most effective way for us to help them on their spiritual journey. I believe participation to be more beneficial than more traditional forms of teaching, learning, mentoring, discipling or any of the other processes we might use to explore spirituality. Indeed, I would go as far as to say that young people's inclusion in their own spiritual development is imperative. Thankfully, a growing number of youth workers have recognised this.

> '...Established institutions are not good at coping with this new approach to common life and decision making. It appears to be chaotic, time consuming and open to abuse. Those who are used to exercising power as if it were their natural right become frustrated when the group process allows even the most reticent participants a chance to contribute. The goal, however, is not efficiency but inclusion. The process is a reaction against the way in which people (especially those marginalized through nonconformity with norms) have previously been excluded and their voices silenced.'
> (The Prodigal Project – Journey into the emerging church, *Mike Riddell, Mark Pierson and Cathy Kirkpatrick, SPCK 2000, pp26,27*)

The following few pages will take a look at why the participation of young people is important, why young people's participation might be desirable and, finally, what some young people have said themselves about participation. It is intended that these thoughts will encourage those who work with young people to reflect on their practice in terms of how well they are including young people themselves in their own development – physical, emotional, psychological and spiritual.

Then and now

God's community

From the beginning of Scripture, God seems to be drawing our attention towards and endorsing the importance of community. 'Let us make man in our image', flows from a united decision of the Godhead to create a being which is made in his multiple image and indeed indicates that an evil relating to a lack of community is present in the world before the fall (that is if you accept that 'not good' can be interpreted as evil) 'It is not good that man should be alone' (Genesis 2:18). Indeed the usual word used for God in the Old Testament, is Elohim – a word that is written and expressed as a plural. God seems to continue this predisposition towards inclusiveness and participation by relating to communities through leaders who are to connect with nations, families and groups. Many of the Old Testament prophets were called to speak to the *people* of Israel as a group/community/nation.

Jesus – the group worker

Jesus continues this mode of operation by working within the context of groups. He often seems to be actively encouraging participation:

▌ He uses open-ended and effective questions like, 'Who do you say that I am?' (Luke 9:18–20) 'Which one of these was a real neighbour to the man who was beaten up?' (Story of the good Samaritan, Luke 10:25–37)

▌ He gets people to reflect on their surroundings, 'Do you see these stones?' (Luke 21:6) 'He saw a fig tree.' (Matthew 21:19)

▌ He gets them to try things out for themselves with instructions like, 'You feed them.' (Luke 9:13) 'Go to the people of all nations.' (Matthew 28:19) 'Follow me.' (Matthew 4:19)

Jesus was a gifted group worker! He knew well that those he was seeking to develop needed individual attention from him, as well as time to work things out for themselves through group discussion, group process and their own experience. He knew that the spiritual, academic and theological insights that he offered would need to be practised and reflected on, particularly through experience. Eugene Peterson puts it like this in his rendition of Matthew 7:24:

> 'These words I speak to you are not incidental additions to your life... they are foundational words, words to build a life on. If you work these words into your life you are like a smart carpenter...'
> (Peterson, E. 1993)

Look again at the way he sent his young disciples out into the world in Matthew 10. He offered them a clear set of instructions, they had received some background theory (via the Sermon on the Mount, which we read in Mathew 5–7) and then they were taking part in the Kingdom as well as hearing about it. The question that I want to raise is: are we involving young people effectively in our youth programmes, in their own spiritual development, in our mission, in our local and national expressions of church?

Interesting perspectives

Interestingly, I sit typing this chapter at a well-known Christian festival. As I write, a young person knocks on the door. He has been sent to clean my room – a dismal task! I tell him that the room is OK, but thank him for asking. We strike up a conversation and he asks what I am typing. He is interested that I am writing a chapter for a book and asks if he can read it later on. I say, 'Sure' and am tempted to leave it at that, but the inner voice says, 'You're writing about participation – mightn't he have something to say to the people that will read this?' So I explain about the piece that I am writing and ask him, 'What would you like to say to people from churches about young people and how they can be more effectively involved in the life of the church and their own development as Christians?' His reply is typical of the wisdom and insight that I find in so many other young people who I have tried to listen to in my own spiritual journey. It is with his permission, then, that I share his thoughts:

'A lot of people in church don't respect the views of young people. People who don't go to church slag it off, but they need to find themselves. Everyone has a bit of God, if we listened maybe there would be less conflict?'

If we listen? If we involve young people? God knows we need less conflict. Important questions and statements which need a reply from those of us who are working amongst young people. Another young person, who is involved in youth work herself, wrote to me recently when I asked her to write what I have called an 'epistle from the edge' to the church. My intention with these 'epistles' is to publish them in the future as letters to remind the church of the voice of young people and youth workers. In her letter, she captures some of my hopes and fears about the future participation of young people in our church situations well:

'As a youth worker and young person I feel very strongly that the church shouldn't limit the younger generations. I am constantly amazed as I watch God working powerfully with children as young as seven. I know ten-year-olds with a deep true faith. We need to be challenging this generation not feeding them puréed Bible stories.

No wonder the church is losing its youth, we are not stimulating them, and we are not helping them find the answers they are looking for. In all things we must be sincere, as a generation we have lost faith in authority, in government, in the media, in the police and justice system, in the education system and in the church.

Everywhere we look we see manipulation and self-interest, plastic smiles and hidden problems. For once we want people to start being real. We don't care that things are not perfect; we can respect someone who admits they have a problem.

Don't prejudge our problems. We are as diverse as you with a whole range of issues that we struggle with, not just the ones highlighted by the media. In all things don't make young people feel immature, respect their viewpoint on life. They are younger and will inevitably

*have less experience in many areas (but not all) of life. Seek to
help us mature instead of making us feel inadequate.*

*In summary meet each age at its own level. You have been our
age, we haven't been yours. If you revisit where we are at, you may
be surprised at how much you learn and how much you see of the
glory of God.'*

She expresses things we avoid at our peril: we need to practice processes
and methods which make the platitude 'young people are the church
of today' into a reality. Please note that I do at least acknowledge that
some have left behind the notion that 'young people are the church
of tomorrow'. Sadly, many Christians have not. I often wonder what
our families, communities, society, church and the world would be like
if we perceived these arenas as borrowed from our future rather than
inherited from our past? The compact disc of resources, which
accompanies this book, is offered as a resource in making the
participation of young people in their own spiritual development more
effectual.

In case you need to be convinced of the value of involving young
people more effectively in their own spiritual development, let me
offer you some reasons for including young people in the process of
developing their own (and our!) spirituality. I do so because I want
you to know that it is in all of our interests to be those who think and
act in participative ways.

Why participation?

We need their voice

Firstly, let me say that we should not include young people in the church
and their own spiritual development out of a well-meaning sense of
paternalism. The Scripture teaches us that,

*'In the last days, God says, I will pour out my Spirit on all people.
Your sons and daughters will prophesy, your young men will see
visions; your old men will dream dreams. Even on my servants
both men and women...' (Acts 2:17,18)*

One of the main reasons that we should seek young people's participation is because we need their sense of vision. It has often occurred to me that God has in this Scripture provided a wonderful model for church development. It is a model in which the dreams of the old (often the subconscious versions and reviews of our past) are in a dynamic relationship with the visions of the young (the thoughts of what might be possible in the future). Theoretically at least, it is a harmonious recipe for church governance and development, one that requires consideration by so many churches that are dominated by the views and agenda of those of us who are older!

Involvement promotes ownership

I was struck by the views of a youth worker in Glasgow, who was telling me about a youth facility that he and other local people ran with and for young people. Despite the 'social deprivation and poverty of that community', he reflected on the fact that in three years the youth project had not lost anything, had no graffiti and was still reasonably tidy. In his opinion, the local young people felt they owned the building. They had decorated the building, they used it and were represented in the management structure of the project. It is not difficult to translate the value of ownership into the arenas of spiritual development – wouldn't it be great if young people perceived their own, and other people's, spirituality as something which is for them and not done to them.

Participation is an effective way of learning

Alan Twelvetrees picks up on this theme in looking at the way in which community work is partly about informal processes of education and learning. Twelvetrees states:

> 'You have to try to help people not to make too many mistakes but learning by doing, which is what community work is about, inevitably involves some mistakes.' (p80)

A brief reflection on our own capacity to learn might help to convince us, if we need convincing, about the importance of participation in effective learning. Have you remembered and learnt more from what ~~ heard, read or experienced?

Participation is exciting

Based on my experience of lecturing and my observation of others who teach, I estimate that a participatory activity needs to be built in at least every 10–20 minutes! How many lectures have you sat through with a growing sense of fatigue and boredom? Note-taking may help, even doodling, but in the end we run the risk of making learning, development and education a tiresome chore. On the other hand, authentic and relevant participation and experiential activity seem to be a tonic in most of the learning scenarios I have been a part of. Perhaps the most interesting and creative way of making this point is offered in a cautionary tale recounted by Mike Riddell in his book *Threshold of the Future*:

> *'A certain flock of geese lived together in a barnyard with great high walls around it. Because the corn was good and the barnyard was secure, these geese would never take a risk. One day a philosopher goose came among them. He was a very good philosopher and every week they listened quietly and attentively to his learned discourse. "My fellow travellers on the way of life",* he would say, *"can you seriously imagine that this barnyard, with great high walls around it, is all there is to existence?*
>
> *"I tell you, there is another and a greater world outside, a world of which we are only dimly aware. Our forefathers knew of this outside world. For did they not stretch their wings and fly across the trackless wastes of desert and ocean, of green valley and wooded hill? But alas here we remain in this barnyard, our wings folded and tucked into our sides, as we are content to paddle in the mud, never lifting our eyes to the heavens which should be our home."*
>
> *These geese thought that this was very fine lecturing. "How poetical," they thought. "How profoundly existential. What a flawless summary of the mystery of existence." Often the philosopher spoke of the advantages of flight, calling on the geese to be what they were. After all, they had wings, he pointed out. What were the wings for, but to fly with? Often he reflected on the beauty and wonder of life outside the barnyard, and the freedom of the skies.*

And every week the geese were uplifted, inspired, moved by the philosopher's message. They hung on his every word. They devoted hours, weeks, and months to a thoroughgoing analysis and critical evaluation of his doctrines. They produced learned treatises of the ethical and spiritual implication of flight. All this they did. But one thing they never did. They did not fly! For the corn was good, and the barnyard was secure.' (pp70,71)

It is a young person's right to be involved

Our government's acceptance of The United Nations Convention on the Rights of the Child, 1989, introduces for the first time a legal obligation upon adults to listen to and include children and young people. Article 12 of The Convention, states:

'States Parties shall assure to the child who is capable of forming his or her own views the right to express those views freely in all matters affecting the child, the views of the child being given due weight in accordance with the age and maturity of the child'. (The UN Convention on the Rights of the Child – Adopted by the UN General Assembly on 20th November 1989 and entered into force in the UK in 1992.)

I don't want to enter into an in-depth discussion on the 'rights of the child' debate in this chapter. My own commitments and beliefs are aligned to the notion that God is just, protects and promotes the rights of the weak, oppressed and helpless (see for example, Isaiah 1:10–17 and chapter 58). I believe that God calls us to live a radical alternative lifestyle which turns many of the prevalent values in our society on their head (see for example, Matthew 5–7).

Young people's experience

For the last three years, I have been spending time doing some investigation and research into the subject of participation and young people. The research has been carried out in collaboration with young people and the focus of the research has been young people's participation in decisions. Some 24 young people have worked on this research with me over three years, and a further 230 young people have helped by taking part in small-group exercises and questionnaire completion.

The research looked at children and young people's awareness and experience of their right to participate, particularly in the decision-making process. It also explored those things which young people identified as helping them to participate more effectively.

It is a good thing that we are all different, but so often our differences can lead to division and separation rather than the increased richness and diversity which are so much part of God's Kingdom. Many young people in the church have felt excluded because they are different, and many have left the church. They have often not been involved in the life of the church. It is perhaps time that a closer look was taken at these differences and what appropriate responses adults can make to help young people feel more included. Many children and young people feel left out. Those who work with young people and the church face a unique opportunity to demonstrate inclusive forms of relationships across the generations.

> Many young people in the church have felt excluded because they are different and many have left the church. They have often not been involved in the life of the church.

Inclusion – an optional extra?

I don't see this type of inclusion as a marginal activity in terms of our spirituality, it should not be an optional extra which some Christians might seek to model for the rest of us. I would argue that it is central to the gospel message and its relevance to the world. I suggest that inclusion and the potential for all to take part in the church is an expression of love. The Bible teaches us that all will know we are his disciples – if we have love for one another (see John 13:35).

A good question to ask at this point is, 'How do we feel when we are left out?' You might like to pause in your reading and remember a specific time when you were left out, when you couldn't participate in a situation that you thought you should have been able to. List your feelings, list any actions that you took and then think about the outcomes. Look back on your list with the knowledge that young people are no different from you. They too feel frustrated, angered, helpless, annoyed, put down, excluded, apathetic and any other emotion that you may have listed. They, too, resort to resignation, hostility, deviance, defiance, violence, withdrawal or any of the other actions that you may have listed. The difference between them and us is that we may be more mature in terms of being reconciled to the emotional consequences of exclusion. What are the implications of being left out of your own spiritual development?

My conversations with young people have largely confirmed that they are often excluded or marginalised in the decision-making process, and that this occurs for a wide range of reasons. Young people cite their own beliefs and behaviour as factors that both prevent and enhance their opportunity to participate. However, they also stress the importance of adult perspectives, attitudes and behaviour in relation to their ability to take part in decisions. It was important for me to come to know that young people accept responsibility for their own opportunities to participate and this was endorsed by my findings. This raises the question, will we, as adults, accept any responsibility for their exclusion?

> They stress the importance of adult perspectives, attitudes and behaviour in relation to their ability to take part in decisions.

What is childhood and youth?

In thinking about young people's participation, our own understanding and assumptions about childhood and youth are important. Many sociologists would suggest that the terms 'childhood' and 'youth' are not definitive and widely agreed concepts but are rather terms that have been constructed in a historic, social and political context.

Our understanding and definitions of childhood and youth will affect how we see them and might well result in inappropriate attitudes and behaviour towards them as people. It is all too easy to label someone in a particular way and then apply our own attitudes and feelings towards them. This way they end up neatly boxed, so that we feel satisfied but they do not. Definitions of childhood are complex. Received wisdom, or 'common sense', seems to suggest that everyone knows and agrees what childhood is, how children should be treated and the types of behaviour that can be expected of them. Exceptions to 'the rules' are often the subject of particular attention.

Sifiah Yusof is 13 years old and she recently started a maths degree at Oxford University. The wide-ranging extent of media interest which followed her story illustrates how young people are often 'labelled'. If they do not conform to this labelling they can so easily become mariginalised. She and her family received media attention that was of freakish sideshow proportions. Closer examination of the attitudes of adults, in the many differing roles where they relate to children and young people, reveals anything but a clear definition of childhood or consistency of understanding, attitude and behaviour towards them.

Pause again in your reading and think about those things that have influenced your own understanding of 'childhood' and 'youth'? How have your attitudes towards young people affected the way that you relate to them? Do you think that you work from any unnecessary assumptions? How might these assumptions affect the way in which you explore young people's spiritual development with them?

James and Prout (1990) provide a degree of clarity about the complex nature of childhood and youth when they suggest:

> '...it is biological immaturity rather than childhood which is a universal and natural feature of human groups, for ways of understanding this period of human life – the institution of childhood – vary cross culturally although they do form a specific structural and cultural component of all known societies. (p3) ... Childhood is a variable of social analysis. It can never be entirely divorced from other variables such as class, gender or ethnicity. Comparative and cross cultural analysis reveals a variety of childhoods rather than a single and universal phenomenon.' (p8)

Current discrepancies in understanding, attitude and behaviour that adults and wider society demonstrate towards children indicate that there is no singular, or definitive, approach to childhood. Children and young people encounter a mismatch of expectations and experiences from the different adults and adult institutions that interface with their lives.

A wide range of age-related anomalies exist. A well-documented one is the fact that young people in the UK can go to war at the age

Figure 1 The ladder of participation

Taken from *Children's Participation: from Tokenism to Citizenship* Roger Hart, UNICEF 1992

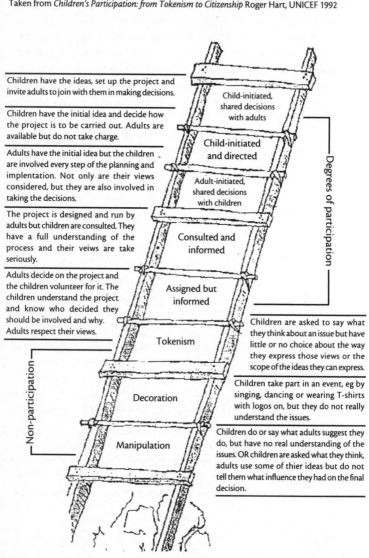

Children have the ideas, set up the project and invite adults to join with them in making decisions.

Children have the initial idea and decide how the project is to be carried out. Adults are available but do not take charge.

Adults have the initial idea but the children are involved every step of the planning and implentation. Not only are their views considered, but they are also involved in taking the decisions.

The project is designed and run by adults but children are consulted. They have a full understanding of the process and their veiws are take seriously.

Adults decide on the project and the children volunteer for it. The children understand the project and know who decided they should be involved and why. Adults respect their views.

Child-initiated, shared decisions with adults

Child-initiated and directed

Adult-initiated, shared decisions with children

Consulted and informed

Assigned but informed

Tokenism

Decoration

Manipulation

Degrees of participation

Non-participation

Children are asked to say what they think about an issue but have little or no choice about the way they express those views or the scope of the ideas they can express.

Children take part in an event, eg by singing, dancing or wearing T-shirts with logos on, but they do not really understand the issues.

Children do or say what adults suggest they do, but have no real understanding of the issues. OR children are asked what they think, adults use some of thier ideas but do not tell them what influence they had on the final decision.

of sixteen on behalf of a government that they cannot vote for until they are eighteen. They are assumed to be able to take responsibility for any crime committed at the age of ten and yet they are not deemed responsible enough to own a pet until they are twelve! Less well known are some of the hidden anomalies, for example, at what age should children choose how they dress, be consulted on a family house move, choose what they watch on television, or be involved in the process of their spiritual development?

Goldson (1997), a sociologist, identifies some of the social mechanisms and events, which have been important in terms of determining adult perceptions of childhood, from a historical perspective. He traces a complex interplay of social, economic, political and cultural factors which have shaped and influenced the concept and experience of childhood considerably. If you are interested in further exploration of this sociological theory it is well worth further in-depth reading. He points out:

'...childhood is not a static, objective and universal fact of human nature, but a social construction which is both culturally and historically determined.' (p2)

An alternative formulation of childhood might start from the position that children are socially competent rather than incompetent unfinished objects of social engineering. Wyn and White (1997), who have looked at the way society views 'youth', articulate well the importance of being aware and balanced in such perceptions:

'The challenge, in rethinking youth, is to maintain a balance between recognising the importance of physical and psychological changes which occur in young people's lives and recognising the extent to which these are constructed by social institutions and negotiated by individuals.' (p12)

Space does not allow a comprehensive description of the issues and considerations relating to sociology's views of childhood and youth. These thoughts are offered as a brief introduction, which you may want to explore further. My own learning has led me to attempt to conduct my research in collaboration with young people. One tool that I have found helpful throughout the research has been Roger Hart's 'Ladder of Participation'.

...at what age should children choose how they dress, choose what they watch on TV, or be involved in the process of their spiritual development?

It has been useful for me to reflect on the way in which young people have been involved in my research by reflecting on the ladder's differing rungs. Where do you place yourself in terms of the involvement and participation of young people? Hart (1997) points out that adults need not assume that the ladder of participation that he has developed is a kind of incremental ideal:

> 'The ladder of children's participation is not meant to imply that a child should always be attempting to operate at the highest level of their competence. The figure is rather meant for adult facilitators to establish the conditions that enable groups of children to work at whatever level they choose. A child may elect to work at different levels on different projects or during different phases of the same project. Also some children may not be initiators but are excellent collaborators.' (p41)

Hart goes on to stress that the important issue is that adults should never operate at the bottom three levels of the ladder, which are manipulation, decoration and tokenism.

Helping young people participate

If we are interested in increasing young people's participation, how might we go about it? My exploration of this subject with young people reveals how we might respond to this question.

Figure two outlines the range of factors that young people identified in my research that would help them to be able to participate more effectively. These are the factors which were most frequently mentioned by young people. Young people seemed as aware of the term and importance of 'responsibility' as those adults who often quote it whenever 'children's rights' are mentioned. Many of the factors that are mentioned in Figure two are to do with areas of personal responsibility. Some areas are the young person's own responsibility, others may be deemed those of adults. For example, factors like communication skills, acceptance of individuality, respect and motivation might well be defined as personal responsibility.

Young people were also aware of a wide range of 'external' factors, which could be deemed as largely outside of their control, that would help them to participate, for example, adults listening, encouragement, resources and being taken seriously. Figure two also indicates the importance of the group or peer, context for participation, demonstrated by the fact that 'group unity' and 'friends taking part' are given a high priority.

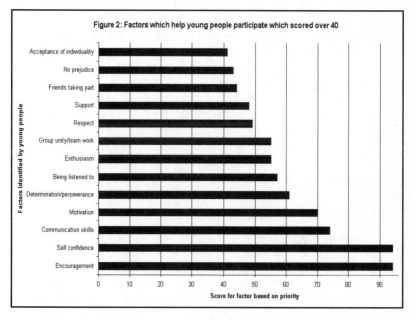

Figure 2: Factors which help young people participate which scored over 40

It is worth reflecting on our own practice by using this diagram. The factors which these young people identified as a priority, in terms of helping them to participate effectively, raise some good questions about our practice:

▌ Do we offer enough encouragement and do we do it authentically, without patronising young people?

▌ How do we promote self-confidence and generate motivation?

▌ How do we know that the young people we work with feel listened to by us?

- Are we effective communicators and can we create and sustain enthusiasm?
- What kind of support do our young people require to participate effectively?

There were many occasions in my research when I observed the well-documented phenomenon of peer influence. One small group of young people that I was visiting was despondent and withdrawn at the stage of the research that involved completing a questionnaire. It appeared that one group member was influencing the others. Through negative comments and body language, she made clear that she was unwilling to participate. On this occasion, one of the young people from the group that worked with me throughout the three years was also present. She joined the group, offering another perspective of the research, and eventually inspired the group's enthusiastic involvement. I observed the transformation of the group's attitudes from a distance, noting how the older girl took temporary leadership of this group of younger girls. She explained the value of the research and how it might help young people participate in adult-dominated decision-making processes.

The importance of peer relationships

It is important for those seeking the effective inclusion of young people to ensure that consideration is given to the potential of young people to facilitate participative processes themselves. As Tisdall and Hill (1997) have indicated, parents and other adults are often concerned about peer relations and influence. My research would indicate that their comments about the potentially positive nature of peer relationships are as valid:

> 'Peer support and communication plays a vital positive role in learning about the world and developing a personal and social identity ... Peer relationships embody conflict and differentiation as well as harmony and integration. For peer networks this results in cleavages and hierarchies, whilst for individuals it has implications for status, acceptance and self-esteem.' (p98)

Some personal reflections

My time spent with young people over the last few years has led me to a range of more personal discoveries.

Firstly, as the research progressed I remembered, and became increasingly conscious of, a range of experiences that I had had as a young person which had excluded me from decision-making processes that affected my life. It seems to me that inclusion is an important element of human development, which has lasting and deep emotional associations. This statement resonates strongly with my own notions of spiritual development – how can we think of helping young people to develop their spirituality in any other way than one which includes them in the process?

It is also worth noting that my relationship with my own children evolved throughout the research process as I became more consciously aware and active in relation to their right to take a more comprehensive role in family decisions. To assess the effect of this in my family life would require some discussion with my children and wife. My own observation is that it has led to many discussions and some tension for my wife and I as we share differing and evolving perspectives on areas of decision-making within the family. This may be important for those of us who work with young people as there is an inevitable relationship between our 'public' and 'private' worlds.

Secondly, whilst planning to increase the participation of young people in an activity, it is possible to become paralysed by the ethical and pragmatic details. The phrase 'good enough participation' enabled me to progress with my research when I was challenged by more idealistic notions of perfect inclusion. It was important to act imperfectly and reflect on learning rather than remain paralysed by idealism. It is most important to remain open to change throughout any participative process with young people. A model of behaviour, which includes planning together, acting together, reviewing and evaluating together in a recurring way, is best practice.

> It seems to me that inclusion is an important element of human development, which has lasting and deep emotional associations.

Lastly, mutuality and reciprocity are key aspects of working in groups, whatever the age of those concerned. They have seemed an increasingly important aspect of human relations to me. Looking back on the three years of involvement with this group of young people, it is clear to me that their contributions and involvement have transformed my expectations. An important aspect of this has been willingness to give and take responsibility, to be open about questions and concerns, to remain open to learning and to listen.

Summary of findings

The conclusions of my research are not substantiated in any depth here, but they arebriefly set out as factors that could be considered in relation to our work with young people on their spiritual development.

Young people are both able and interested in contributing to and participating in social research. Careful negotiation of role and involvement is important and adults who might be involved in the research process need to remain aware and open about their own role and interests. Whilst this statement is directly related to research, I believe it is also applicable in the context of spiritual development. Are we aware of our own agenda in helping young people to develop their spirituality?

> Are we aware of our own agenda in helping young people to develop their spirituality?

Young people have many ideas about how adults can improve the way in which they are included in decisions. It is important to enter into dialogue with young people about their inclusion This means that we need to consider young people's involvement in the process of considering their spirituality when the temptation might be to collaborate only over questions of content.

Some young people are more aware of their rights than others. Those who are more aware of their rights may be less dependent on the interpersonal dimension of shared decision-making. This has implications about how we work in groups. Those who are less aware of their own rights may rely more on others' involvement.

Young people do not identify age and maturity as being important in terms of their potential to be included in decisions. Whilst these factors may be of significance to adults, and particularly adult legislators, they are not factors which young people appear to have prioritised as crucial to participation. The challenge is not that children must be sufficiently developed to take part in decisions, but rather that adults need to be well developed enough to find ways of including children and young people. We should not have a linear view of development, which is age related, but rather a view based on shared understanding and negotiation about appropriate inclusion.

Adults need to be aware of the 'feelings' component that young people identify as being important to participation. This is particularly so if they want to involve young people effectively. This requires a degree of sensitivity on the part of adults, which may well be a challenge to views about decision-making that are based upon the competition and conflict which can dominate some adult decision-making arenas.

Young people are generally aware of the responsibility that participation and inclusion places upon them. They identify many factors, relating to the ways in which participation can be improved; often these stress their own need to be responsible. Young people are aware that there is a kind of 'internal' responsibility, that they have within themselves, which balances with an 'external' responsibility that adults have to exercise when involving young people.

Young people seem most disappointed with their opportunities to participate in school and are keen that this should change. It is worth noting that this finding is in relation to the six other contexts explored in my particular research (ie family, national politics, local politics, health, neighbourhood and the media). This is important for those of us who are exploring spiritual development in the context of schools.

Young people are interested in political involvement. However, their current experience of it is not positive.

Young people express most satisfaction about their ability to participate in their home context. They are also generally positive about their participation in health.

Young people are not aware of the UN Convention on the Rights of the Child. What is possibly more concerning is that they do not perceive themselves, in terms of many of the social contexts explored in my research, as exercising those rights. It does not appear that the government has fulfilled their obligation under Article 42 of the Convention to make young people aware of the rights afforded them by the Convention.

The young women and girls involved in my research generally have higher expectations of participation than young men or boys. No direct explanation for this observation is possible with regard to the results of the research as it was not the focus and a follow up inquiry might be of use. However, it is worth noting that young people identified issues like 'acceptance of individuality', 'no prejudice' and 'respect' (see Figure two) as high priorities in terms of factors which help young people participate. I would suggest that there is a link between these statements and the possibility that sexism and discrimination might be perceived as a priority reason for low participation. Young women and girls are increasingly aware of this, for example, as a result of the development of the women's movement. Their higher expectations concerning participation might be a result of this raised awareness.

Working class young people in this research generally expressed lower expectations and ambitions regarding participation than more middle class young people (housing and employment were used as indicators of class). Again, no direct explanation for this observation is possible, as it was not the focus of the research. However, it is worth noting the factors identified by young people in this research as high priorities in terms of helping them to participate effectively. The second and third highest factors identified by young people were 'self-confidence' and 'communication skills' respectively. I believe that these two factors could be identified as having a potential relationship to social class and the notion of class injustice. It could be argued that the characteristics of those in 'higher social classes' include the use of more elaborate language, higher educational achievement and greater self-confidence. These are characteristics that link directly to the factors of 'self-confidence' and 'communication skills', which were identified by young people in my research. A predisposition, based on social class, not to be as able to exercise these factors could arguably restrict ambition and expectations on the part of working class young people to participate in decisions.

Black young people in my research generally expressed a greater degree of dissatisfaction with their opportunity to participate in a range of contexts. Their expectations and ambitions regarding participation tended to be higher than white young people's are. The contemporary context of my research abounded in public debate and concern about individual and institutional racism in the UK. Events, discussion and public awareness surrounding the tragic death of Stephen Lawrence were an example of the degree of intense consideration being given to racism by some. I believe that my research underlines the dissatisfaction that many black young people would express about the degree of opportunity to take part in decisions in the UK. It is further suggested that black young people's expectations and ambitions regarding participation tend to be higher and that this is underlining a growing movement of discontent and challenge to this lack of opportunity, a movement which is not displayed by their white peers. A cultural sensitivity to the way in which we seek to involve young people is critical in any context where we seek increased participation. I would want to argue that this is particularly true relating to young people's spirituality.

Maintaining momentum

Phil Treseder (1997) identifies a helpful checklist of things to remember when working with children and young people on their increased participation, as you reflect on your own performance in this area it is a good list to consider:

- Be honest.
- Listen to criticism.
- Be open and approachable.
- Keep a sense of humour.
- Treat children and young people with respect.
- Do not patronise.
- Do not prejudge.
- Be non-judgemental.
- Learn from mistakes.
- Take account of children and young people's needs.
- Be flexible.
- Do not expect children and young people to lavish you with thanks. (p 39)

Hopefully, this will have offered you some insights into the importance of including young people in their own spiritual development. This awareness, and the resources on the compact disc which comes with this book, should be a real help to your work with young people.

References

Goldson, B 'Childhood: an Introduction to Historical and Theoretical Analyses,' in Scraton, P (Ed) *Childhood in Crisis*, UCL Press, 1997

Hart, R *Children's Participation – the theory and practice of involving young citizens in community development and environmental care*, UNICEF, 1997

Hill, M and Tisdal, K *Children and Society*, Longman, 1997

James, A and Prout A (Ed) *Constructing and Reconstructing Childhood: Contemporary issues in the sociological study of childhood*, The Falmer Press, 1990

Peterson, E, *The Message*, Navpress, 1993

Riddell, M *Threshold of the Future – Reforming the church in the post-christian west*, SPCK, 1998

Riddell, M, Pierson, M and Kirkpatrick, C *The Prodigal Project – Journey into the emerging church*, SPCK, 2000

Tresseder, P *Empowering Children and Young People – Training Manual*, Children's Rights Office and Save the Children, 1997

Twelvetrees, A, *Community Work*, BASW, 1982

Wiles, D *Taking Part in Decisions: Collaborative research with young people exploring their knowledge, experience and views about their right to participate in decisions*, University of Bath, 2000

Wyn, H and White, R *Rethinking Youth*, Sage Publications, 1997

Other related reading

■ *All Together Now – Community participation for children and young people*, Save the Children Fund (SCF)

- *Building small Democracies,* Gerison Lansdown
- *Changing Places – Children's participation in environmental planning,* Adams and Ingram
- *Children's Rights and Participation in Residential Care,* Carolyne Willow
- *Children's Voices in School Matters,* ACE
- *Empowering Children and Young People – Training Manual,* SCF
- *Empowering through Social Skills,* John Huskins
- *Hear! Hear! – Promoting children and young people's participation in Local Government,* Carolyne Willow

Creativity

Creativity

Jo Pimlott

In the beginning

God is creative

> 'In the beginning God created the heavens and the earth.' Genesis 1:1

From these opening words of the Bible through to the end of Revelation, we are shown a God who is essentially creative in nature. He speaks and the world springs into being. A creation unfolds which is diverse, imaginative, incredibly detailed and wonderfully held together. In his dealings with mankind, he is infinitely creative in the way he communicates:

▌ He seals his promise to Noah with the visual sign of a rainbow *(Genesis 9)*.

▌ He speaks face to face with Moses, whose face glows so brightly afterwards that he has to cover it with a veil *(Exodus 34)*.

▌ He causes a donkey to speak to confront Balaam with his wrongdoing *(Numbers 22)*.

▌ He attracts Elijah's attention with wind, earthquake and fire and then speaks to him in a gentle whisper *(1 Kings 19)*.

▌ He sends a hand to write an inscription on King Belshazzar's wall *(Daniel 5)*.

▌ He sends a fish to swallow Jonah to get him back on track *(Jonah 1)*.

▌ He sends angels to speak to Hagar, Balaam, Gideon, Mary and many others.

▌ He communicates through dreams and visions to prophets, kings and ordinary people.

Jesus – our model communicator

If we take Jesus as our model for communication, discipleship and teaching, we begin to see the same creativity emerge. In his teaching, he consistently uses storytelling, object lessons, parables, brain teasers, imagery, practical demonstrations, involvement and participation. He changes his approach depending on his audience at any particular time. He responds to questions with an explanation, a story or still more questions. He is the master of the down-to-earth and yet the master of imagination. We are shown, through the gospel accounts, how the disciples and, in other contexts, the crowds who flock to him listen transfixed, and go away enlightened, amazed, puzzled or questioning. To us in the Christian church, who so often like to give clear pat answers, Jesus is an enigma – often quite content to send the crowds away to work the answers out for themselves. We need to have the courage, not only to study his methods, but also to take them, adapt them for use in our culture and begin to risk using them.

The creative juices

A visual age

'Imagination is more important than knowledge.' Einstein

A recent survey discovered that 85 per cent of American teenagers watch MTV on a daily basis. (New World Teen Study quoted in Naomi Klein's *No Logo*). This generation of young people is one that is visually driven. Even music no longer stands in its own right, but is increasingly dependent on the pop-video to enhance its appeal. The generation of young people we are working with are accustomed to having their senses appealed to, tickled and tantalised.

Today, more than ever, we live in a culture which is incredibly creative and diverse. Creativity surrounds us – from the worlds of television, film, advertising, popular music, computing, games, fashion, etc. Educationalists are increasingly realising the importance of encouraging creativity and creative thought. Visual images are recognised to be as important, if not more important, than the spoken word. Millions are spent on intricately woven together television advertisements, engineered to touch the senses and the soul. Music videos have become a means of storytelling and firing the imagination. Interactive computer games absorb more and more of a young person's time and focus. Used to being bombarded with visual image after visual image, young people are no longer content with sitting and listening.

Hindrances to creativity

> 'Creating is not the same as making. You can make a bed, but you have to create a garden. Making is what manufacturers do. Creating is what poets and lovers do. Nothing was ever created that didn't have a piece of the creator in it.' Mike Riddell

We serve a creative God, we follow a creative Master, we live in a creative culture, yet often Christians seem to trail behind in these areas. We, who should be at the forefront of innovation and creativity, reflecting the heart of our Father, so often seem to be locked into specific ways of doing things. Frequently the spirit of 'how we do things round here' appears to dominate. Fear of change, fear of making mistakes, fear of looking stupid, fear of losing control, fear of becoming too worldly stops us from exploring and pushing back the frontiers of creativity.

Some of these fears are justified. Creative approaches are higher risk approaches: there is more danger of things going wrong, there is a need for more planning, thought and preparation. The advantages, however, far outweigh any of these. In 1 John 4:18, we are told that, 'There is no fear in love. But perfect love drives out fear, because fear has to do with punishment.' Perhaps we need God to fill us with more of his love, so that our love for Him and for those we are working with, drives out the fears listed above.

Before we look at some practical steps, it is helpful to explore and consider some of the technical background to issues surrounding creativity.

The brain and creativity

Until relatively recently, very little was known or understood about the workings of the human brain. Even as late as the forties and fifties the brain was regarded as being a very simple and straightforward organ, able to process and store information, but limited in its capacity and abilities. Recent research has thrown more light on the workings of the brain, and this is useful in understanding the creative process.

It has been discovered that the brain is divided into two sides, left and right. These sides are similar in biological terms and can even be thought of as two identical brains working in harmony with one another, yet each side of the brain handles different activities. Research carried out by Professors Sperry and Ornstein in California has thrown light on these differences.[1]

The left side of the brain has been shown to handle mental activities such as words, numbers, logic, sequences, lists and analysis. The right side deals with imagination, colour, rhythm, awareness of space and dimension, music, daydreaming and other such activities. Their research has shown that people who have been educated to use one side of the brain to the exclusion of the other are relatively unable to use the other side. Most teaching in the west concentrates on educating and exercising the left side of the brain. Our traditional approaches emphasise the importance of words, numbers, logic and lists. People who are stronger in areas of the right brain are often perceived as less intelligent.

Although it might appear that creative people have a tendency towards a 'right brain' approach, this does not have to be the case. Research appears to show that we all have the capacity to exercise each side of the brain. When the 'weaker' side is stimulated and exercised, there is a significant rise in overall ability and effectiveness.

An interesting example of someone who used both sides of his brain to great effect is Albert Einstein, considered by many to be the greatest scientist of his time. He failed maths at school and was nearly thrown out of college for daydreaming. He discovered his Theory of Relativity not seated in front of a desk, but lying on a hill one summer day letting his mind wander. He used both sides of his brain to great effect, but the trigger to his greatest discoveries was the right side of imagination and creativity. My husband Nigel would not see himself as a naturally creative person. He is much stronger in 'left brain' activities – strategy, logic, analysis. He has, however, through exercising and developing the right side of his brain, learned to think, imagine and work in creative ways.

When we first began to use music, drama and other creative approaches in our work with young people, we struggled with our own preconceptions of what it meant to be 'creative'. In our minds, creative equalled 'arty farty'. We have found that many youth workers have these kind of misconceptions together with the ensuing reluctance to embrace creative ways of working. What we discovered for ourselves, and what we have seen many others discover, is that these kind of creative approaches can be learned and the required skills developed. Many youth workers who do not consider themselves artistic or creative have used them effectively.

Wallas' model of the creative process

Being creative in our approach to youth work enables us to see the bigger picture, discover and explore different viewpoints and find solutions to problems. Wallas' model of the creative process[2] sheds light specifically on how creativity can help in problem solving. He identifies four stages in the creative process: preparation, incubation, illumination and verification. These form a very helpful process by which youth workers can prepare and develop material for use with a group.

Stage one: preparation

The problem, need or desire is defined and any information needed is gathered. This might involve identifying a subject, doing background reading or research, talking to young people about their thoughts, feelings and ideas, or pulling together any available resources.

Stage two: incubation

Time is taken to step back from the problem in order to work it through. This can take minutes, weeks or even years. This stepping back involves imagination and reflection. Thinking can be aided by brainstorming, writing notes, mind-mapping, drawing, walking etc.

Stage three: illumination

Ideas arise from the mind to provide the basis of a creative response. These ideas and thoughts can be pieces of the whole or the whole itself. This stage is often brief, involving a rush of insights within a few minutes or hours. The ideas and insights gained here could provide the heart or framework for an activity or series of activities.

Stage four: verification

There is a need, having reached this stage, to demonstrate whether the illumination works. This is the time to pull together the ideas and put them in a usable format, using the background reading, research and skills as a foundation.

The role of the youth worker

So often the youth worker has been seen as the person with all the answers. There has been an unspoken (or sometimes articulated) expectation that they will have endless biblical revelation, worldly wisdom and experience to draw on. The reality is often far from this. Many of those working with young people are untrained, unqualified and inexperienced. Many work long hours in stressful situations and undertake youth work in their spare time. The youth worker does not necessarily have all the answers but is there to help the young people discover the truth for themselves. The key skill is to help young people undertake learning experiences and to guide them through this learning. Creative approaches which engage the young person's interest and enthusiasm are easily learned and quickly developed. Although these creative approaches still demand a lot of preparation, they can make a small amount of material go an awfully long way.

Many creative techniques, once learnt, can be adapted to all kinds of different situations. The ideas in this book can be taken, adapted and used for work with a variety of different ages, groups, numbers, backgrounds. Once the confidence of the youth worker has grown and they have mastered these techniques, they can adapt, change and vary them to suit all kinds of different situations.

Developing our own creativity

In order to facilitate these kind of approaches, it is helpful for the youth worker to be constantly developing and nurturing their own creativity. These are a few suggestions of things that we have found to be of particular benefit:

- Brainstorming – collect any and every idea and piece of information in the initial stages of developing an idea.
- Mind-mapping – a very useful tool, a kind of advanced brainstorming with words and pictures, developed by Tony Buzan. See *The Mind Map Book*, Tony Buzan.
- Look for multiple solutions – 'Nothing is more dangerous than an idea when it is the only one we have.' Try and think of as many different solutions to a particular problem as possible. Allow your imagination to flow with even the most obscure of ideas. Think the unthinkable.
- Serendipity – the gift of accidental discovery. Meditate, pray, fast, observe creation and don't miss inspiration when it strikes.
- Visit other cultures and people groups – go outside your own comfort zones and learn from others.
- Keep asking – God wants to communicate with us. Ask for more of his creative inspiration.
- Learn from others – seek out those whose creativity you admire, and try to learn from them. Also be prepared to learn something from absolutely everybody you come across. Find people that you can bounce your ideas off.
- Study God's word.
- Get some training – have a go at a creative skill you've never tried before. It's amazing how many courses there are around.
- Play – have fun, try new things, get your hands dirty.
- Write it down – get in the habit of carrying a notebook with you to jot down thoughts, ideas, observations, quotes, stories etc.
- Start with something that will never work.
- Exaggerate – the truth is out there, be bold.
- Persist – 'Genius is one per cent inspiration and 99 per cent perspiration.'

A creative environment

'People support what they help create.' Abraham Lincoln

Our aim as youth workers is to provide opportunities and safe places for young people to realise and express their own creativity, thoughts and ideas. To help them learn 'hands on', by discovery, by experience.

Many creative approaches demand cooperation, team work and mutual support. This can have a very positive impact on a group, drawing them together as they undertake activities and develop relationships of trust, between young people and adults and between the young people themselves. It is important to recognise that this is a process. For some groups, it will be important to begin with the kind of activities which demand a little cooperation and gradually to move on to those which require a high level of working together. Other groups will respond immediately to the challenges presented.

These approaches recognise that young people have a story to tell, experience to draw on and opinions which are valuable. They will sometimes involve us giving over control of a session to the young people themselves. It is they who will determine directions, conclusions and outcomes. This can be frightening for workers who are used to holding a tight rein. It needs wisdom and clarity, but this kind of empowerment can build confidence and enthusiasm with young people. The skills are facilitating, guiding and steering – knowing and learning when to interrupt, when to get something back on course and when to pick up on something which is inaccurate.

Drama

Many youth workers shy away from using drama because they have little or no experience of it themselves. With many groups, however, it can provide a whole range of useful activities for young people, enabling them not only to actively participate in a session, but also to engage physically, mentally and emotionally with the subject matter. The following are all techniques which work well with young people and can be used to explore a variety of issues. Many of these can be linked to a broad range of different stimuli.

The short sketch

This is the most straightforward of all drama techniques. It involves the young people creating a short sketch/play on a particular subject or using a particular stimulus.

Here are a few key practicalities to bear in mind:

▮ Make your instructions clear and simple.

▮ Make sure you are available to help those who are struggling – have a few ideas yourself which you can contribute if needed.

▮ Break down larger groups into groups of between three and five. Encourage short plays with one single scene or impose a time limit.

▮ Simplicity is the key to good pieces of drama.

▮ Ground rules about the use of language or physical violence may need to be established.

▮ Allow time at the end to watch and discuss the sketches. Encourage the group to give feedback on what they have seen.

Some suggested stimuli:

▮ a story

▮ a video clip

▮ a newspaper headline or cutting

▮ a magazine article

▮ a poem or short piece of writing

▮ a picture or a poster on a contemporary issue

▮ a word or phrase

▮ props or costumes which must be used within the sketch

▮ the names of a number of characters

▮ an object

Role play

There are several ways to use role play with young people. A few ideas:

▮ Prepare cards describing different characters. Ask the young people to act out what these characters might do in certain situations.

- Take familiar characters – the young people themselves, characters from television soaps or characters from a Bible story – and ask the young people to act out what they might do in a certain situation.
- Use a problem page letter, poem, picture, cartoon, video clip or virtually anything else as a stimulus for role play.

It is very easy to stay at a surface level with role play, but encourage the young people to think more deeply about the character they are playing. What are their thoughts and feelings in this situation? Why do they say and do what they do? What are their hopes, dreams and motivations? As a slight variation on role play, you could try using role reversal as a technique.

Hot-seating

This follows on from role play, but develops the idea further. It is a technique which is used to explore the thoughts, feelings and motivations of a particular character in more depth. One character takes the 'hot seat' and everyone else asks them questions. If this follows a prepared sketch or role play, the questioners might be asked to stay in character as well as the person being hot-seated. This needs a little more maturity, and works best with groups of young people who have become accustomed to using drama on a regular basis.

If a young person or a number of young people are to be hot-seated, they may need time to think about the character and prepare in advance. Another way of using hot-seating is for one of the leaders of the group to take on a character – someone in a particular situation, with a particular problem, someone who is perhaps wrestling with the issue at the heart of whatever theme you are exploring. They could take on the role of a Bible character in order to present and explain the story to the young people in a creative way. A pre-prepared monologue can be an excellent introduction to this, following which the audience are allowed to ask any questions they want to.

Some tips for effective hot-seating:

- Make sure the characters or their situations are interesting enough to spark curiosity and questions.

- Set out the room so that there is a clear place for the 'hot seat'.
- Have a few questions ready yourself in case things dry up.
- Don't be afraid to tackle both the simple questions: 'Why did you say ...?' and the more complex ones, 'What would you have done if...?'

Mime

Mime is a useful tool and combines well with the use of either dance or music. Use some simple mime exercises as warm-ups for an activity like this. For example, ask the group to mime something they have done during the day, or to mime a particular mood or emotion. For a lengthier activity, give the group a piece of music, a Bible reading, a song, a poem or a combination of these and ask them to create a series of appropriate actions to go with it. Encourage them to think not only of actions which act out something literally, but of actions which are more symbolic. This is a good way of getting young people to think deeper about what the musician, writer, artist is trying to say. Visual images, a picture or video, could also be used for this, or young people could be asked to act out a certain scene in the style of an old black and white movie, with mimed actions and the occasional caption.

A few other ways of using drama

- Give the young people an unfinished script, or show a video clip up to a certain point. Ask them to work in groups to finish the story. This works particularly well with dilemma or cliffhanger type situations, where the group has to make choices or decisions on behalf of the characters. Allow time for discussion afterwards.
- Ask young people to rewrite the end of something. This is similar to completing the script, but the group are shown or told one ending and must come up with an alternative one. This is useful for thinking through the consequences of actions taken.
- Try simulation exercises where the young people are put into a specific imaginary situation and told to act out what happens. This is one step on from role play.

■ Use the bodies of the group to form sculptures, words, pictures or symbols – called body sculpting. This can be done individually, in pairs, small groups or by the whole group working together.

Art and craft

Art and craft activities can provide some of the simplest and most effective hands-on ways to explore issues, stimulate discussion and get young people thinking more deeply about the subject in hand. If these activities are presented in the right way, they can be tackled by anyone – even those who would not see themselves as artistic. They are also very handy to use in a group with a wide age range, as they tend to be accessible to all. It is important to make it clear that the process is as important as the finished product. The aim is not to produce something which is a masterpiece, but to express thoughts and feelings through the process of creating something. It doesn't matter if no one else can tell what it is! An added bonus to the learning process is that the young person often has something to take home with them that will remind them later of what has been said, discussed or explored.

For this style of activity, try to create an environment where people feel safe to have a go. On a practical note, think in advance, not just about what is needed for the activity itself, but what else you might require. Messy activities might call for floor coverings and some form of protection for clothing. Clearing up afterwards might require bin liners, soap, water, cloths and towels. These are things easily forgotten, which can make a big difference to the smooth running of the activity and the stress levels of the youth worker.

Modelling

Use Fimo, clay, Plasticine or play dough. A good activity for people to do as individuals, modelling can be used as part of a meditation or thinking process. Some ideas for starting points:

■ Make something from the natural world which makes you think of God.

- Make a model of yourself.
- Make a model of someone else in the group.
- Read a poem, tell a story or describe a situation and ask young people to make a model of a face which shows how a person in the poem, story or situation feels.
- Model something you saw or did today.

For those with a bit of space or for something to do out of doors, junk modelling/sculpting can also provide an effective modelling activity on a larger scale. If you have more time and access to the necessary equipment and skills, pottery activities also work very well with groups of young people.

Collage

This is a great activity for using up bits and pieces. You can use paper, fabric or virtually anything else you can find. Magazines and newspapers are particularly good because they give words and phrases which can be selected, and the images and words can provide direct links to the young person's culture or experience. Some ideas:

- Create a collage which reflects who you are inside.
- Make a collage which reflects what you think of when you hear the word 'Time' (or take any word, issue or theme you are looking to explore).
- Create individual collages which are then put together in some way to form one large one.

Ask young people to create collages in pairs or small groups or create one as a whole group.

Murals

A painting done directly onto a wall, a mural is a great way to involve a whole group. It is particularly good if you are meeting in a building where something can be left and developed over a number of weeks. Murals can be a permanent way of adding to the decor in a particular room or building, a long-term project which can be very effectively and meaningfully undertaken by a group of young people. Thinking through the content, colour, shape and style of the mural can provide excellent opportunities for discussion, exploration of issues, freedom of expression and ownership for the young people involved. In a very real sense, it is a way of marking out space, and ownership of that space. For those groups who have no permanent building or no opportunity to undertake this kind of project, simpler, short-term versions of this activity can be accomplished using large sheets of paper or wallpaper attached to a wall.

Graffiti wall

A useful way of giving young people the opportunity to express their thoughts and feelings generally or on a specific issue. Wallpaper or large sheets of paper stuck together can form an effective graffiti wall. This works particularly well on a residential, where young people can add to the wall anonymously whenever they wish to do so. The levels of artistic ability might vary considerably and this can be a high-risk activity for those of a sensitive disposition. Freedom of expression will inevitably mean that things will be written and drawn on the wall which you may not welcome. You have been warned! Generally though, as with many of these kinds of activities, the advantages outweigh the risks.

Cartoons

Most young people are familiar with cartoons from comics, magazines, television or film. This kind of activity works well with a broad age range and the results can be made into some kind of magazine or publication. It may be worth buying or borrowing a simple book on cartooning to help the group get started. Alternatively, bring in someone who is good at cartooning to give them some tips.

A few potential starting points for activities:

- Use an existing cartoon and ask young people to draw pictures to complete the strip.
- Ask individuals to draw a cartoon on a particular theme.
- Ask young people in groups to create a cartoon character that would appeal to their generation and then to put them in a cartoon strip on a particular theme.

- Photocopy a humorous cartoon and blot out the captions or words of the characters. Ask the group to make up their own.
- Draw giant cartoons.

Face painting

Simple books are now available which help with ideas for face painting. Although this might often be seen as something that would work better with smaller children, Dave Wiles recounts many fascinating experiences of using face painting with teenagers. This is a group activity and half of the fun is that a group will gather and watch the art happening. It enables people to see themselves differently and can provide opportunities for discussion and in-depth conversation.

Painting and drawing

This might seem an obvious activity, but there are ways in which we can think beyond the rather overused 'draw a picture of this Bible story' approach. We have asked young people to worship using paint and large sheets of paper, with positive results. Particularly for those young people who do not like to sing, this can be a way of allowing them to express their thoughts and feelings towards God. Painting rocks or other objects with symbols or pictures can also be a way of young people expressing their thoughts and feelings. Paint and large sheets of paper on tables or the floor can be used to great effect in all kinds of creative and imaginative ways.

Other art and craft ideas

- Story boards. These are a displayed sequence of pictures which outlines the plan of a film, TV advertisement or similar. Young people can be asked to draw and develop a story board on a particular theme. These could be displayed for their own sake, or used as the basis for drama sketches.
- Make cards. We have made thank you cards to God as part of worship, which worked well, but the year brings with it many opportunities to make cards for specific occasions.

- Potato printing. Have fun with half spuds.
- Screen printing. This is a bit more complex, but worth further reading and investigation, if you want to undertake a more advanced activity with your group.
- Make posters for events, on an issue, or simply for fun.
- Make puppets and use them to act out short sketches.
- Make masks. These are very useful in exploring issues of image, being real and discussing thoughts, feelings and emotions.
- Create magazines or newspapers. This can draw in a variety of different creative skills within a group.
- Collect pictures or visual images to use as stimuli or triggers for other activities or games.

Music

> 'Musical training is a more potent instrument than any other, because rhythm and harmony find their way into the inward places of the soul, on which they mightily fasten.' Plato

Using song lyrics

The lyrics to some chart songs can provide useful starting points. Many of them resonate with young people in terms of their experience or are simply very well known to them. The websites of some bands publish song lyrics, as do popular music magazines.

Use the song and the lyrics in a variety of ways:

- Devise questions to go with them and ask people to work in groups to answer them.
- Use the words of a well-known song alongside the words of a simple psalm then compare and discuss them.
- Encourage the young people to think about the values and beliefs which are hidden behind the words of the song. What emotions or feelings are being communicated? What statements is the writer making about life, love, the world? What attitudes or behaviour are they promoting?

- Ask young people to use their imagination and tell or act out the 'story behind the song'.
- Take well-known song lyrics and ask the young people to rewrite them. How would they overlay their opinions, values or experience? What would be different from the original? What things would stay the same?

Background music

Songs and instrumentals of all different styles can be used to great effect to create an atmosphere for meditation or thinking time. Sometimes young people find complete silence difficult, but music provides a focus and can provide a sense of security. Reading something over a piece of music can help the group focus on what is being read. Showing slides or pictures or silent video clips can add to the effect and communicate a message or stimulate thought in a very powerful way. Choose a piece of music that reflects the mood you want to create. Experiment by using styles the young people would not normally listen to.

Desert island discs

Ask the group to bring in a tape or CD of their all-time favourite songs. Spend time listening to each one and use this as a way of encouraging them to tell their story. What is it about the song that they like? How does it reflect how they were feeling at the time it first came out? Is it linked with any events or memories in their history? Give plenty of time and be sensitive in drawing out information.

Making music

There are many ways of making music with young people. For those with skilled musicians in the group, the temptation is to go for a standard youth band approach, but some of the following are worth a try as well. Performing in front of an audience, whether at a special event or even as part of a church meeting, can be a confidence-boosting experience for a young person. Alternatively, simply use the ideas in a workshop or club type setting. For those with less naturally musical groups, don't be afraid of having a go.

Here are a few starting ideas:

- Use percussion as a means of self-expression. Get hold of some basic percussion instruments and let the young people have a go. Make a joyful noise, experiment with rhythms and beats.
- Make junk music. Encourage the young people to create their own instruments out of junk, then have a go at making music together.
- Create or write your own songs. This is easier with groups who are musical, but not impossible for others. Perhaps you could get a musician or two along to help. Encourage young people to write their own lyrics on a specific theme.
- Write your own raps. This can be fun and relatively easy for those who cannot play instruments or are not keen on singing. Experiment with these, using percussion sounds, whistles etc.
- Have a go at recreating contemporary music. Do a *Stars In Their Eyes* special, where people imitate their favourite performer.
- Try music technology, mixing or using record decks. This can be a useful learning experience and one which many will enjoy. Invite someone to do a workshop or find out if there are studios in your area which cater for youth groups. Some county councils have studios available and workers who are trained in delivering workshops for young people.
- Create your own dance music. Cheap computer software is available to help you achieve this.

Video

Watching video clips

There is a film for almost every subject and they provide an excellent resource for the youth worker who is willing to do the necessary research. Clips from films, adverts, TV soaps, cartoons or documentaries can provide starting points for discussions or exploring an issue. Some drama and art and craft ideas can be triggered by a good video clip.

Some tips:

- Make sure the content is appropriate for the age of the young people who are watching.
- Make sure the clip is neither too long nor too short.
- Be prepared to explain the context of the clip for the benefit of those who have not seen the rest of the film or programme.
- Make sure the equipment you have is sufficient to allow the whole group to both see and hear clearly.
- Set up the equipment and try it out beforehand to save embarrassing pauses in the middle of the session in which the young people watch you wrestle with technology.
- Make sure you have quiet before you start the clip – there's nothing worse than everyone missing the key bit because people are still settling down.
- Ask questions. A quiz afterwards can add to the effectiveness of the clip, particularly if the young people know this is going to happen (and particularly if there is a prize involved somewhere!). This can greatly aid their powers of concentration.

Making a video

This requires good equipment, a responsive group and lots of patience. Have a plan in mind before you begin. The experience for young people of seeing themselves on television is usually a very positive one, but some sensitivity may be needed where there are very shy or reserved members in the group. The whole experience of being filmed is a valuable one and although some may find it just too scary, many young people respond with added enthusiasm and concentration to the task in hand, when they know they are going to be able to watch the finished product themselves later. Do remember to ensure that you have the facilities to play back as well as to record, so as to avoid disappointment.

There are lots of different styles of video which can be made by groups of young people:

- adverts
- video diaries

- an imitation of a popular TV show
- vox pops
- news bulletins
- imitation documentary on a particular issue
- recording of a prepared sketch or drama activity

Games

> *'Play is more an approach to life than an activity in life. Play is already the number one learning experience of postmodern culture.' Leonard Sweet, Soul Salsa*

Hopefully, all these creative approaches will have elements of play in them, but games themselves are very popular, particularly with younger age groups. They often provide a good starting point to a session, drawing the group together and focusing attention. They can be used to relax a group and get them moving and interacting. Lots of activities can be made into games with a little adaptation. Many books of games are on the market and space forbids an extensive list.

These are types of games which have been found to work well with groups of young people in different contexts:

- Some management games are good when exploring issues of cooperation, developing leadership skills, identifying gifts and talents etc.
- Team games and wide games give opportunities for cooperation and working together.
- Trust games done properly can help build relationships in a group.
- Simple games on a theme can provide a really helpful introduction to an issue or subject. For example, a competition to make the best outfit out of two bin bags, two newspapers, six drinking straws, a toilet roll and a roll of sticky tape could lead on to activities focusing on fashion and image.
- A quiz on a theme, eg true or false questions to link in with a discussion on reality and truth.

- Games about everyday dilemmas, eg 'What would you do if...?' can link into a theme.
- Music or video quizzes.
- Issue-based quizzes. Many local authorities or county councils have health resource libraries which can provide interactive quiz games on issues like alcohol, drug awareness and sexual health.
- Taking well-known shows, eg *Who Wants to Be a Millionaire*, and adapting them.
- A growing number of games specifically designed for use with young people are now available, like 'The Road' and 'The Fast Game'.

Storytelling

We spend our lives surrounded by stories. As well as being very familiar with stories, many young people genuinely enjoy them. They read them, they tell them and they watch them being acted out in the form of films and television programmes. Storytelling is a way of engaging not only the mind, but the imagination as well. Storytelling helps us connect our world, our values and ideas to those of other people. Stories carve out a meeting place where the emotions can be touched. In the church, we often seem to forget that the Bible is a collection of stories, not a theology textbook – it is about people with real lives, real struggles, grappling with real issues. Many of the stories have great relevance to young people today. This amazing book has stories about love, sex, murder, bribery, corruption, marriage, rape, alcohol abuse, power, poverty, homelessness, refugees, illegitimacy, peer group pressure and virtually every other issue you could imagine.

Stories provide one of the greatest resources for the youth worker. In addition to the wealth of stories in the Bible, it is helpful to collect and store stories. Look out particularly for those that will connect or resound with the young people you are working with. Good sources for stories include television, magazines, newspapers, books, the Internet, personal contacts and your own experiences.

Some keys to effective storytelling:

∎ Think about the wider context of the story. Try to recreate the setting or atmosphere. Consider sights, smells and sounds. Create mental pictures for the listener to visualise. These images are the things which are likely to stay in the memory the longest.

∎ Identify the conflict or struggle in the story. This is one of the key structural parts of the story, creating shape, structure, interest and tension. Conflicts can be those between characters or perhaps inner conflicts like the pull between courage and cowardice or the battle between good and evil. The ending of the story should draw this conflict to some kind of resolution.

∎ Think about the feelings and emotions in the story. Identify the currents of feeling which motivate the characters. Often the meaning of the story comes from these.

∎ Write the story down and practise 'performing' it several times. Think carefully about the meaning of each word and check that you understand what each phrase and sentence is saying. Experiment with tone, volume, pauses etc. Practice on someone and ask for feedback and suggestions.

Some suggestions for creative storytelling:

∎ Use objects, pictures or slides as visual aids while telling the story.

∎ Tell the story from the point of view of one of the characters.

∎ Ask those listening to perform specific actions or sound effects whenever a specific character or word is mentioned.

∎ Tell an older story in a modern setting or context.

∎ Rework a famous story and give it a twist.

Other creative techniques to explore

Space and time do not allow us to fully explore the subject of creativity. By its very nature, this is a flexible subject and individuals will no doubt be able to add extensively to the ideas covered here. Further examples of creative approaches are listed below. Some of these link in with ideas already discussed, others would demand skilled input from a specialist helper or further learning by the youth worker:

- events – fashion shows, makeovers, sleepovers
- fund raisers
- discussions/debates
- dance
- outdoor pursuits activities
- exploring nature
- sports
- guided journeys
- karaoke
- poetry
- writing letters
- problem page letters and answers
- circus skills – juggling, unicycle, clowning etc
- and many, many, many more.

A note about copyright. When using material written or developed by others, for example, music, books, video etc, check the copyright information on the article. You may need to get permission to use it.

Maintaining momentum

We started our journey by looking at God's creativity. For me, the incarnation demonstrates the ultimate in creative communication. Jesus becoming a man is all about God speaking to the world in a language the world can understand. If we are to effectively communicate the heart and mind of God to those we are working with, we need to engage with their culture and find appropriate ways of exploring the gospel for this generation. Creative approaches enable us to give young people ownership of the learning process; they provide opportunities for experience and imagination and for the use, expression and development of creative gifts.

The question, 'When was the last time you did something for the first time?' is the one which springs most readily to mind as I draw these thoughts to a close. It is so easy for us to stagnate and become entrenched in particular ways of working – to stay within our own 'safe zones' and to rely on tried and tested methods or particular familiar resources. If we are to work creatively, we need to invest time, energy and imagination. We also need to draw from what is within us – from our own ideas, experiences, questions and dreams. This can put us in a vulnerable position but can also help us, perhaps more effectively, to learn with and from the young people.

Creativity is at the heart of the very nature of God. I do not believe it is an optional extra or something simply for those out on the fringe. If we are to work effectively with young people, we need to work creatively.

Footnotes

[1] *Make the most of your Mind*, Tony Buzan, Colt Books 1977

[2] *The Creative Brain*, Ned Herrmann, Brain Books 1988

About the writers

Nigel Pimlott is the coordinator of the Connect Spiritual Development Project. He has worked with young people for over 15 years, having done extensive schools work, church-based youth work and youth-worker training. Nigel is on the Centre for Youth Ministry National Council, Spectrum Board, and is a voluntary-sector representative for Nottinghamshire Connexions. He is concerned about how the church treats young people and is a passionate supporter of Manchester City Football club.

Jo Pimlott is an assistant church minister/youth worker and has worked with young people for 15 years. She has a passion for training, developing and releasing people into their destiny. Her work tutoring and training youth workers is highly regarded and exploring creative approaches lies at the heart of her work. Jo sits on several regional and national youth work boards and planning groups. She is currently studying for an MA in Training and Theology. When not working you are likely to find her either covered in paint or immersed in a crime novel.

Dave Wiles is the Chief Executive Officer of Frontier Youth Trust. He has 26 years of experience in youth and community work and believes that this has far greater street cred than the fancy MPhil he has just obtained at Bath University! Dave worked for the Children's Society for 21 years in a wide range of roles and contexts having come into youth and community work as an apprentice to Bob Holman (Easterhouse – Glasgow), following a turbulent adolescence! He says that youth work is great 'helper therapy' on the basis that he is still working out what happened to him in the 60s and 70s! His favourite learning style is participative – and he usually ensures that this is voluntarily compulsive!!

CD-ROM

The contents of the accompanying CD are provided "as is" and without warranties of any kind, either express or implied. Scripture Union does not warrant or make any representations regarding the use or the results of the use.

To the fullest extent permissible pursuant to English law, Scripture Union disclaims all warranties, express or implied. Scripture Union does not warrant that the functions and links to external websites contained in the materials available on the CD will be uninterrupted or error-free, that defects will be corrected, or that the materials available are free of viruses or other harmful components. You (and not Scripture Union) assume the entire cost of all necessary servicing, repair and correction.

Under no circumstances, including but not limited to negligence, shall Scripture Union be liable for any special or consequential damages that result from the use of, or the inability to use the CD even if Scripture Union has been advised of the possibility of such damages.

Furthermore, Scripture Union do not warrant to provide any technical support on the installation or use of this CD, nor on the computer(s) on which the CD is used.

You are advised that Scripture Union is not responsible for the functionality or content of any external website. Although all hyperlinks were correct at the time of going to print, Scripture Union cannot guarantee that these references will remain valid.

Your statutory rights under English law are not affected.

Before running the CD-ROM you are advised to read the readme.txt file located on the disk.

On the attached CD-ROM you will find over 100 ideas that were originally available as five separate A4 resource books. The CD-ROM has been created to be used with any frames-enabled Internet Browser, such as Internet Explorer 4 or above and Netscape Navigator 4.7, or above. To print out accurately the handouts and visuals you will need Adobe Acrobat Reader installed. This is a free piece of software and is downloadable from a link found on the CD-ROM.

The CD-ROM should run after being inserted; however if it doesn't, click the CD-ROM icon on your desktop and then click on the start.htm file.

Requirements:

CD-ROM drive
Frames-enabled Internet Browser
Adobe Acrobat Reader
Printer (recommended)
Modem with Internet access (recommended)